THE USBORNE SOCCER SCHOOL
TRAINING AND FITNESS

Jonathan Miller

Designed by Stephen Wright

Illustrations by Bob Bond

Photographs by Shaun Botterill (Allsport UK)

Edited by Gill Harvey • Managing editor: Felicity Brooks

Consultants: John Shiels, Bobby Charlton Soccer Schools Ltd.;
Nasira Sheikh, National Museum of Science and Industry (London)

With special thanks to players Nathan Brooks, Nicola Burton, Leanne Davis, Rachel Horner,
John Jackson, Lindsey Jamieson, Matthew Rea, Mohammad Usman Shafiq, Ciaran Simpson,
Mark Travis, and to their coach, Gavin Rhodes.

Photographic manipulation by John Russell • American editor: Peggy Porter Tierney
Additional design work by Michèle Busby and Zoe Wray

CONTENTS

TRAINING BASICS

To be a good soccer player, you must be fit. The best way to develop a high level of fitness is to do regular training sessions. Working out can be tough, but it is also very rewarding and it helps you improve your soccer skills, too.

GETTING AN EDGE

An out-of-shape team has no chance of winning against a fit one. Regular training can improve your all-around ability and can make your team difficult to beat. It gives you the edge over opponents in the following key areas:

Speed – you can get past opponents more easily and be first to the ball.

Stamina – you have enough energy to play a whole game at your best.

Strength – you can win the ball in tough challenges to turn defense into attack.

Quick reactions – you can anticipate play and punish opponents' mistakes.

TRAINING AND ENERGY

Your body has two ways of producing the energy that you need when you exercise – the aerobic energy system, and the anaerobic energy system. These terms appear throughout the book. Here is an outline of how both systems work.

The anaerobic system provides a lot of energy quickly but can only work for short periods of time.

The aerobic energy system is what you use when you do steady activities such as walking or jogging. It uses your food and the oxygen you breathe in to create energy in your muscles. The harder you exercise, the more oxygen your muscles need. You breathe deeper to take more oxygen in, and your heart beats faster to pump it to your muscles.

The aerobic system can provide energy for long periods of time.

You use the anaerobic energy system for sudden, 'explosive' exercise such as sprinting and jumping, when your body needs more energy than it can get aerobically. This system does not need oxygen to produce energy, so it only uses your food.

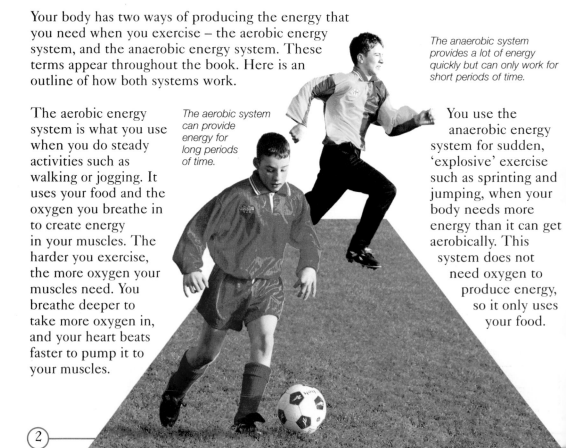

CLOTHING AND EQUIPMENT

If you have the right clothing, you can train in all weather conditions and on different surfaces. Wherever you train, try to keep warm.

Sports markers, such as those shown here, are useful but not essential. You could use bags or sweaters instead.

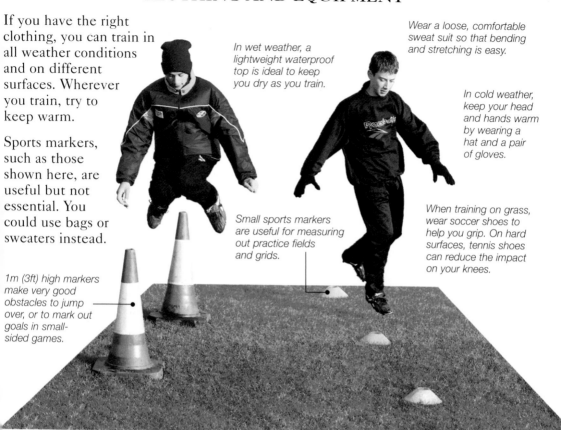

In wet weather, a lightweight waterproof top is ideal to keep you dry as you train.

Wear a loose, comfortable sweat suit so that bending and stretching is easy.

In cold weather, keep your head and hands warm by wearing a hat and a pair of gloves.

Small sports markers are useful for measuring out practice fields and grids.

When training on grass, wear soccer shoes to help you grip. On hard surfaces, tennis shoes can reduce the impact on your knees.

1m (3ft) high markers make very good obstacles to jump over, or to mark out goals in small-sided games.

PLANNING A TRAINING SCHEDULE

Plan to train about twice a week, but avoid very hard training in the day or two before a game. Here is an outline of how to structure a session:

Try to make each session varied and interesting. A good training schedule should include aerobic and anaerobic exercise as well as skills work.

10 minutes	First, loosen up for about 5 minutes (see pages 6 and 8), then do some stretches (see pages 7, 8 and 9).
10 minutes	For the next 30 minutes, do a variety of games and exercises. Spend about 10 minutes on each one. There are plenty to choose from in this book. For example:
10 minutes	★ Running games (pages 12-13) ★ Skills training (pages 18-19)
10 minutes	★ Quick reaction games (pages 20-21) Rest briefly between each exercise.
25 minutes	Play a game of soccer (a small-sided game if there are only a few of you).
5 minutes	Warm down for 5 minutes with some gentle jogging and stretching exercises.

This team is doing a variety of activities.

These players are working on their sprinting speed.

Some players are stretching their muscles.

These two players are working on their ball control.

MUSCLES FOR SOCCER

Your body has over 600 muscles. Whenever you do a different activity, such as walking around or running, you use a different set of muscles. Playing soccer uses a wide variety of them. If you know how your muscles work, it will help you to understand how to look after them and how to make them stronger.

WHAT MUSCLES ARE MADE OF

Muscles are made up of lots of long, thin cells or fibers. There are two types of fibers. One is used in aerobic exercises which need stamina, such as jogging. These are called 'slow' fibers. The other type, 'fast' fibers, work anaerobically and provide short bursts of energy. The number of fast and slow fibers in each muscle varies from person to person.

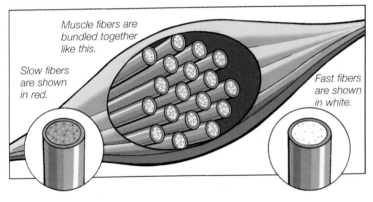

Muscle fibers are bundled together like this.

Slow fibers are shown in red.

Fast fibers are shown in white.

BUILDING STRENGTH

To build up the strength of a muscle, it needs to be worked at full capacity. As you exercise the muscle, its fibers become bigger to cope with the extra work. See page 10 for some strengthening exercises.

Most top professional players, such as Colombia's Faustino Asprilla, have very strong leg muscles.

HOW MUSCLES WORK

Muscles are attached to your bones by flexible cords called tendons. As you use a muscle, the tendon pulls on the bone and makes it move.

Muscles are also very flexible and can contract, or shorten, to half their normal length. A muscle becomes firmer and thicker when it is contracted.

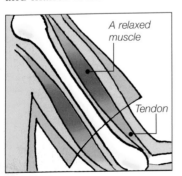

A relaxed muscle

Tendon

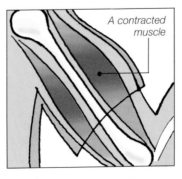

A contracted muscle

KEY MUSCLES

When you are playing soccer, you use many different muscles to run, kick, head or catch. Here are some of the key muscles you use, and what you use them for.

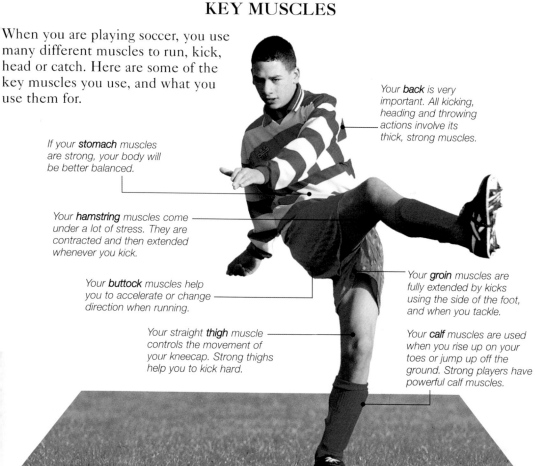

Your **back** is very important. All kicking, heading and throwing actions involve its thick, strong muscles.

If your **stomach** muscles are strong, your body will be better balanced.

Your **hamstring** muscles come under a lot of stress. They are contracted and then extended whenever you kick.

Your **buttock** muscles help you to accelerate or change direction when running.

Your straight **thigh** muscle controls the movement of your kneecap. Strong thighs help you to kick hard.

Your **groin** muscles are fully extended by kicks using the side of the foot, and when you tackle.

Your **calf** muscles are used when you rise up on your toes or jump up off the ground. Strong players have powerful calf muscles.

INJURY RISKS

Most muscles are arranged in pairs which work together when you move. For instance, when you sprint, your hamstrings contract as your thigh muscles extend. If one muscle contracts too quickly, the opposite muscle may be pulled or strained.

In any soccer game, you have to make sudden twisting and stretching movements. This makes it likely that you will get injured from time to time. There are many different ways of injuring yourself, but you can help reduce the chances of this happening (see page 29).

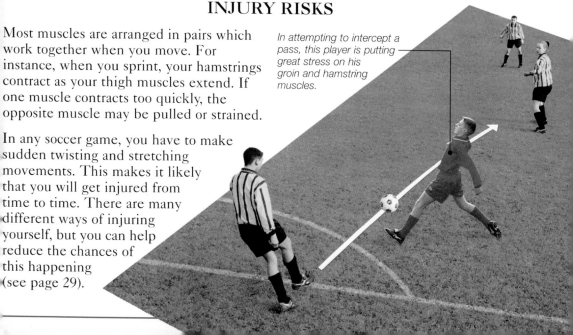

In attempting to intercept a pass, this player is putting great stress on his groin and hamstring muscles.

LOOSENING AND STRETCHING

Every training session should begin with loosening up exercises, because cold, stiff muscles can easily be injured. You should then move on to more demanding muscle stretches. Regular stretching sessions will help you to stay flexible and supple.

GETTING LOOSE

Loosening routines should involve gentle body movements and should raise the temperature of your muscles. It is really important to loosen up your whole body, not just your legs. Once you are warm, you are then ready to try out other exercises and stretching positions which make your muscles work harder. Any loosening session need only last for about five minutes.

Stand with your legs 60cm (2ft) apart and put your hands on your hips. Slowly swing your hips around in a circle five times.

Stand with your feet 30cm (1ft) apart and gently swing your right arm over your shoulder ten times. Repeat with your left arm.

Lie down and raise your right leg up toward your chest. Then lower it and do the same with your left leg. Try not to lift your head up.

JOG AND PASS

To complete a loosening up session, gently work your lower body muscles with some basic ball work.

Jog across a field, and back again, with a couple of your teammates. As you run, turn and pass a ball to each other.

As you jog, try to maintain a gentle, even pace. Don't sprint or make sudden movements.

UPPER BODY STRETCHING

Stretching routines do more than just warm up your muscles. By stressing and extending your muscles, they also increase your flexibility. Only attempt stretching positions after loosening up.

The position shown here stretches your stomach, back and arms. Lie face down and place your hands in line with your shoulders. Use your arms to push the top half of your body up.

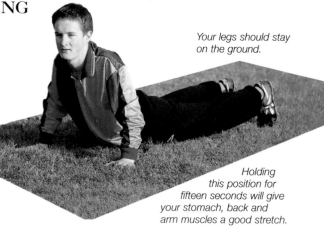

Your legs should stay on the ground.

Holding this position for fifteen seconds will give your stomach, back and arm muscles a good stretch.

CATCH AND THROW

This game is a good way of stretching your stomach. Stop if you feel any tightness in your muscles.

Raise your legs as you catch.

Sit on the ground with your legs slightly bent. Ask a teammate standing about 2m (6ft) away to throw you a high catch. Rock back as you catch the ball above your head.

Throw the ball straight back, pushing yourself forward as you throw. Try to work quickly, changing roles regularly.

STRETCH AND BEND

This is a fast-moving game that stretches your lower back, stomach muscles and the backs of your legs.

Stand back-to-back with a teammate, about 60cm (2ft) apart. Raising your arms right up, pass a ball back over your head to your teammate.

Your teammate should take the ball and then bend forward, passing the ball back to you through her legs. Bend your knees as you take the ball.

A SIDE STRETCH

To stretch the muscles in your sides, swivel around to pass the ball behind you using both hands. Twist one way to pass and the other to receive.

LEG MUSCLE STRETCHING

You use the muscles in your legs for every aspect of soccer, so it is important that you pay particular attention to stretching your lower body. Concentrate on working your hamstrings, groin, thigh and calf muscles.

LEG LOOSENER

Always remember to loosen up thoroughly before stretching. You can use this varied jogging routine as an alternative to 'jog and pass' (see page 6). Place four markers on the ground about 20m (66ft) apart, then start jogging slowly from the first marker to the second. Turn sideways and sidestep to the third marker. Then do another half turn and jog backward until you reach the final marker.

20m (66ft)

Slow jog   Sidestep   Jog backward

Once you reach the end marker, repeat the stages back again to complete the circuit.

Do about three circuits, but don't tire yourself out.

HAMSTRING STRETCH

It's easy to pull your hamstring muscles, so use this routine to help keep them supple and flexible.

A supple player may be able to roll the ball all the way down to the ground.

With your feet together, hold a ball against your chest. Begin to roll it down slowly toward your toes. Bend as the ball moves down, then roll it back up to your chest. If you feel a tightness in the backs of your legs as you bend, don't stretch any farther.

FIGURE EIGHT MOVE

This difficult ball passing routine is ideal for working your groin muscles.

The ball should make a figure eight pattern as it passes around your legs.

Lean over to your left and right as the ball moves between your legs.

Stand with your knees bent and your legs well apart. Swing your right hand around the outside of your right leg to pass a ball to your left hand in between your legs. Then swing your left hand around your left leg to pass the ball back again.

HOPPING GAME

This game is good for stretching your front thigh muscles as well as strengthening your legs and testing your balance. Mark out an area about 3m (9ft) square. Ask two other teammates to play with you.

Bend your right leg back until you can hold it in your right hand. Hop around in this position and try to knock the other players off balance. Play for about one minute before resting. Then do the same holding your other leg.

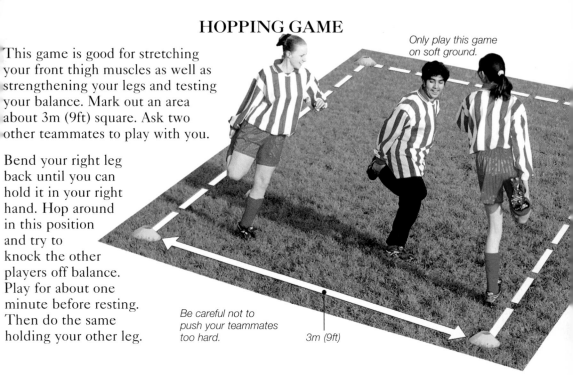

Only play this game on soft ground.

Be careful not to push your teammates too hard.

3m (9ft)

CALF MUSCLE PUSH

You can either do this simple stretching position with a teammate or on your own against a wall.

Push against your teammate for up to twenty seconds, then swap legs.

Place one foot about 60cm (2ft) in front of the other and point both feet forward. Put your hands on the shoulders of your teammate and as he leans his weight forward, push against him. You will feel a stretch in the calf of your back leg.

ANKLE AGILITY

Your ankle joints get a lot of use during a game. They are put under particular stress when you tackle or shoot. Improving the flexibility and movement in your ankles can be achieved with some simple ball control exercises.

Place two markers about 1m (3ft) apart, and drag a ball across from one marker to the other using your instep.

When you reach the other marker, use the outside of your foot to drag the ball back again. Try to work quickly.

To exercise your calf muscles as well as your ankles, rise up on your toes and do quick passes between your feet.

STRENGTH AND POWER

To make tackles or firm challenges for the ball, or to produce sudden, explosive pace, you need to be strong and powerful. When working on your strength and power, make sure you focus on your upper body as well as your legs.

LEG AND BODY LIFTS

This game will strengthen your stomach muscles. Play with a friend and concentrate on working well together, so that you coordinate your movements properly. As it is tiring, take regular breaks.

Your teammate must keep his legs bent.

Lie down flat and hold the ankles of a teammate lying behind you with his feet on your shoulders and his arms stretched out.

With a ball between your feet, raise your legs up. Your teammate does a sit-up at the same time and takes hold of the ball.

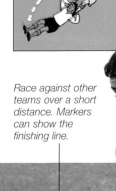

He then lies down again before sitting up. Lower your legs almost to the ground before raising them to get the ball.

Race against other teams over a short distance. Markers can show the finishing line.

WHEELBARROW WALKING

This strengthens your arms and shoulders. Lie face down with your hands on the ground and ask a teammate to lift up your legs. Walk along on your hands with your teammate supporting your lower body.

This player should hold his teammate's feet firmly.

Change over each time you reach a marker.

This player should bend his knees slightly.

HOP AND JUMP CHALLENGE

Hopping, jumping and skipping are good ways of improving the strength and power in your legs. To increase your power, do this exercise as fast as you can, with only a very short time on the ground between hops and jumps. Put a marker on the ground. 5m (16ft) away, put four low markers in a line, 1.5m (4.5ft) apart. Another 5m (16ft) away, line up four 60cm (2ft) high markers, 1.5m (4.5ft) apart. A friend should stand by the final high marker with five balls.

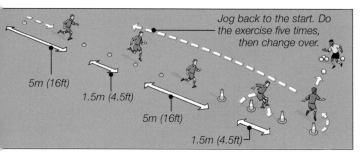

Jog back to the start. Do the exercise five times, then change over.

5m (16ft)

1.5m (4.5ft)

5m (16ft)

1.5m (4.5ft)

Jog from the first marker to the low markers. Hop between the low markers, changing your hopping leg each time.

Jog to the high markers and leap over them using both feet. Once over the last marker, head a ball thrown by your friend.

When you reach the high markers, bring your knees right up as you jump over them.

Keep your eyes on the ground as you land.

ROPE SKIPPING

This is an enjoyable way of warming up your muscles and building up strength in your legs. Try a variety of skipping styles to exercise one or both of your legs.

When you jump over the rope, like this, try swaying from side to side as you skip to develop a rhythm.

When you step over the rope, swap your front leg regularly to give both your legs an equal workout.

JUMPING TIPS

★ As jumping and hopping are quite strenuous activities, it is vital that you warm up properly first.

★ Always use a soft surface such as grass or matting when jumping and hopping, to reduce the impact on your knees.

★ Try using tennis shoes on very dry grass as you may slip over if you wear your soccer shoes.

★ Make sure that this part of your training session doesn't last too long. One ten-minute jumping session a week is enough.

SPEED AND STAMINA

While power in your legs is important, as a soccer player you also need to develop speed and stamina. All players must work on their running skills, but depending on what position you play in, you may need to give extra time to do speed or stamina work.

SPRINTING TECHNIQUE

There are times when you will have to run as fast as you can, whether you play in defense or attack, so knowing how to 'sprint' (run fast over a short distance) is essential. Sprinting uses your strength and power and fully extends your leg muscles.

Swing your arms backward and forward in time with your strides.

Keep your neck and shoulders relaxed and steady.

Your goal is to maximize your stride length. Lift the heel of your back leg up high.

Move your back leg forward quickly, lifting your knee right up. Keep breathing deeply.

Drive your front leg forward and fully extend your back leg. Your stride is now very wide.

Keep your feet and knees facing forward. For extra power, swing your arms vigorously.

CIRCLE SPRINT

The piggy-back position is good for strengthening your leg muscles.

This game improves your sprinting. You need an even number of players. Get into pairs, piggy-back style, and form a circle 6m (20ft) wide.

On a given signal, the player being lifted jumps down, races around the circle, and gets back onto his partner's back. Change positions with your partner after three races.

DISTANCE RUNNING

To build up your stamina, you need to run longer distances at a constant, steady speed. This sort of running can be boring, so it is good to run with other teammates so that you can encourage each other. Put two markers about 40m (130ft) apart.

40m (130ft)

Run at about half your fastest pace.

Stand next to one of the markers with two teammates. One player runs between the markers seven times and then rests while the others run. Next, each player runs six times. Continue this until each player only makes one run.

FOLLOW THE MOVING TARGET

This game is a tough and challenging way of doing steady speed running. Mark out an area about 30m (98ft) square. One player, the 'moving target', stands on the opposite side of the square to the other runners, who are the 'chasers'.

Everyone starts running. The chasers try to catch up with the target runner. If they succeed, rest, then change the target runner. If they don't, stop after five minutes anyway and rest, then change the target.

This is not a sprinting game, so both target and chasers should run at a steady pace.

WHO NEEDS TO RUN FAST?

Most attacking players, such as strikers and wingers, need pace and acceleration over short distances to get away from defenders and to run to through balls.

Here, French international Youri Djorkaeff uses his speed to launch a dangerous attack.

WHO NEEDS STAMINA?

Central midfield players who link defense with attack have to work particularly hard and need a good level of stamina. Full backs and wing backs also cover a lot of ground up and down the wings, supporting attacks and then tracking back to mark opponents.

This full back has covered a lot of ground to get back and tackle his marker.

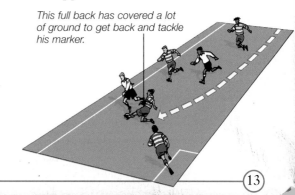

INTERVAL TRAINING

Interval training combines fast running with recovery periods at regular intervals. It is similar to game play where you do anaerobic activities such as sprinting, and aerobic activities such as jogging, in quick succession.

BEATING FATIGUE

During a game, your body often can't get enough oxygen to your muscles to produce all your energy aerobically. This means it has to produce some energy anaerobically (see page 2). A by-product of the anaerobic system is lactic acid which builds up in your muscles. Lactic acid can affect your performance, because it makes you feel tired (fatigued) and makes your muscles feel heavy. Interval training helps you get used to tolerating the build-up of lactic acid.

This player has been badly affected by fatigue and is unable to beat his opponent in this race to the ball.

MARKER SPRINT

This game includes sprinting with recovery periods of slow jogging. Mark out a 20m (66ft) square and put five randomly-spaced markers inside. A few friends should train with you. Each chooses a number and slowly starts jogging around the square.

20m (66ft)

Four players jogging

When you or your coach shouts a number, that player should sprint into the square and touch all the markers, then rejoin the back of the jogging group. End the game when you have all sprinted three times.

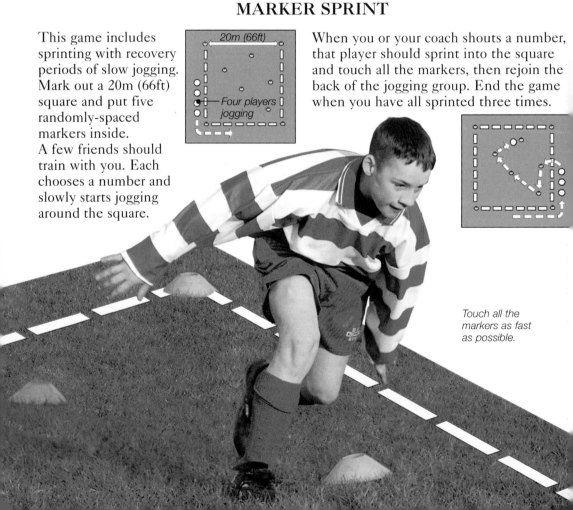

Touch all the markers as fast as possible.

SHOOTING RACE

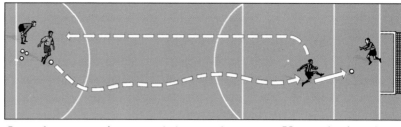

This interval training game also provides dribbling and shooting practice. Play with three or four teammates and your team's goalie if possible. Play on half a full-size field, or use a marker as a starting point and mark out a goal 6m (20ft) wide, about 25m (80ft) away.

One player goes in goal. The others go to the center circle with a ball each. One player runs at the goal and shoots,

and then sprints back. The second player starts once the first has had his shot. Award one point for each goal.

Use gathering the balls as your recovery period.

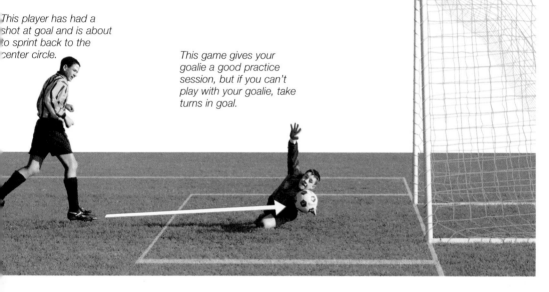

This player has had a shot at goal and is about to sprint back to the center circle.

This game gives your goalie a good practice session, but if you can't play with your goalie, take turns in goal.

INTERVAL TRAINING TIPS

High intensity training makes your heart beat fast, to supply extra oxygen to your muscles (see page 2). If you make your heart work hard on a regular basis, it gradually becomes stronger. As a result, the time you need for recovery decreases.

★ Always give yourself a good recovery period between anaerobic exercise sessions. Although interval training can be hard work, you shouldn't tire yourself out.

★ If you do some interval training about once a week, your body will adjust more quickly to the pace of a game.

STAR FITNESS

It is important for top players to have the same level of energy throughout a game. Here Argentinian striker Gabriel Batistuta moves forward energetically even though it is close to the end of the game.

BALL GAMES

Getting fit is hard work. To make it more interesting, it helps if you include several ball games in your training program as well as basic running routines. These ball games will give you a good but enjoyable workout.

RELAY GAME

This relay race is played in pairs. It combines some ball work with some fast running. Place one marker on the ground, then mark out a circle about 6m (20ft) away from it all the way around. Split into pairs. Each pair should have a ball and stand around the circle.

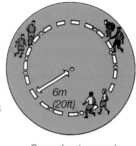

Spread out around the circle.

Try not to kick the ball too far ahead of you.

Dribble the ball toward the marker, trying to go as fast as possible. When you reach it, turn around and start running back toward your partner.

As you run, focus on speed rather than ball skills.

When you get close, pass the ball quickly to your partner who then runs to the marker. The winners are the first to complete five relays.

PRESSURE PASSING

This is a fast game and can give you an intensive workout. Play with about six of your friends. Form a circle 8m (26ft) wide around one central player. Two players around the circle should have a ball.

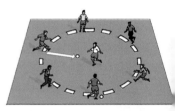

One of the players with a ball passes it toward the center of the circle. The player in the middle receives it and passes to a different player. Just as this pass is made, the player with the second ball passes into the middle.

Keeping two balls on the move is hard work.

The central player has to run quickly backward and forward to provide passes to the rest of the circle. He should change with another player after one minute.

POSSESSION GAME

This game involves a circle of players, with one in the middle. The aim is to make the central player work hard at gaining possession of the ball. No one should be in the middle for more than a minute. Players can change over once they feel tired.

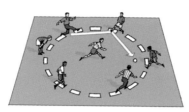

Accurate passes are needed in this game.

Form a circle about 10m (33ft) wide and start passing a ball to each other. Try not to let the player in the middle touch it. If this player intercepts your pass or manages to tackle you, then you must take over in the middle.

ONE AGAINST ONE

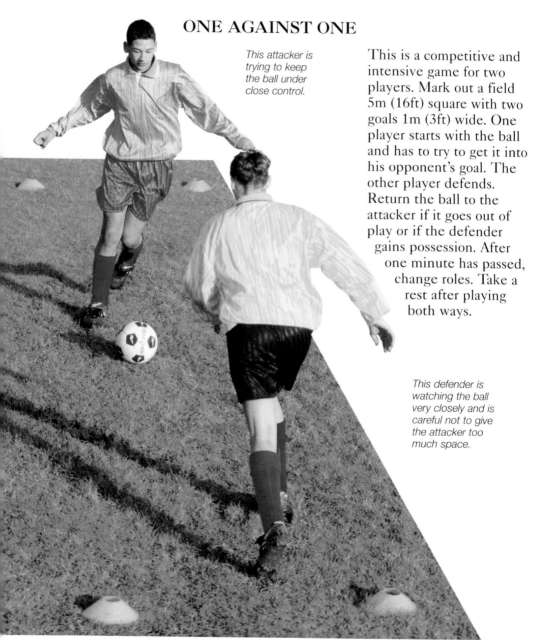

This attacker is trying to keep the ball under close control.

This is a competitive and intensive game for two players. Mark out a field 5m (16ft) square with two goals 1m (3ft) wide. One player starts with the ball and has to try to get it into his opponent's goal. The other player defends. Return the ball to the attacker if it goes out of play or if the defender gains possession. After one minute has passed, change roles. Take a rest after playing both ways.

This defender is watching the ball very closely and is careful not to give the attacker too much space.

SKILLS TRAINING

A good training session should include some skills practice, and there are many ball games which can help improve your playing technique. Concentrate on different skills each time you train.

PASS AND FOLLOW

This game involves quick, accurate passing and some sprinting. Play with at least five teammates and line up in two groups behind two markers, about 8m (26ft) apart.

This player is running to the back of the opposite group.

This player is waiting for her turn.

8m (26ft)

One player passes to another at the front of the opposite group. He then sprints after his pass and joins the back of the other group. Each player continues this pattern. Take a rest after five minutes.

THREE SKILLS GAME

This game needs at least six or seven players. It is useful because it covers throw-ins, ball control, dribbling and some running. Put three markers in a triangle 10m (33ft) apart. Divide the players into two groups, A and B. Group A stands at marker 1 and group B at marker 2. Each player in group A has a ball.

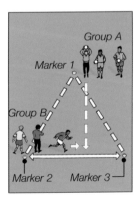

Group A

Marker 1

Group B

Marker 2   Marker 3

A player from group A does a throw-in. A player from group B runs and controls it.

The group B player dribbles around marker 3, as shown, then runs to the back of group A.

The thrower runs to the back of group B. Meanwhile, the next two players repeat the game.

TWO GOAL CHALLENGE

This game tests your shooting skills. You need two other players and three balls. Mark out two goals facing each other, 6m (20ft) wide and 18m (59ft) apart.

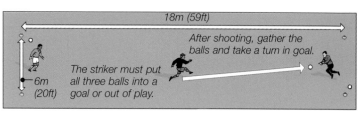

18m (59ft)

The striker must put all three balls into a goal or out of play.

6m (20ft)

After shooting, gather the balls and take a turn in goal.

One player is the striker and has a ball at his feet. The other two players are goalies. Each has a spare ball by one of his posts.

The striker can shoot at either goal at any time. If he scores or shoots wide, the goalie throws his spare ball out to him.

If the goalie catches the shot, he throws the same ball out again. If the ball rebounds out, the striker shoots until it is out of play.

HEAD VOLLEYBALL

This game is good heading practice. Mark out a 6m (20ft) square with a row of markers halfway across it. Play with a friend who stands opposite you. One player throws a ball to the other, who heads it back. Keep heading until the ball falls to the ground. As well as trying to beat your opponent, have some good rallies too.

6m (20ft)

You get a point if your opponent heads the ball outside the grid, or if it drops on his side. The winner is the first player to ten points.

This player is practicing powerful headers by trying to head the ball over his opponent.

The other player is watching the flight of the ball closely and is ready to move back quickly.

MENTAL AGILITY

All good soccer players need to be able to make quick decisions and be alert at all times, so it is important to spend some time strengthening your mental agility. Your reactions are like any other skill – they improve with practice.

SHADOWING GAME

This game helps to develop your powers of concentration. Put ten markers an equal distance apart in a 6m (20ft) wide circle.

Play in threes. Two players stand at opposite markers, while the third player stands nearby, ready to give instructions.

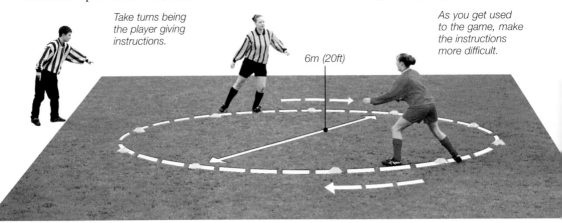

Take turns being the player giving instructions.

6m (20ft)

As you get used to the game, make the instructions more difficult.

The third player shouts out instructions such as 'Move two markers to the right!' The other players follow these instructions quickly. If the players in the circle get the instructions right, they will always be opposite each other. The first one to make a mistake must run around the circle before continuing the game.

DIAMOND GAME

This game tests your mental agility as you need to do the opposite of what is asked. Four players form a diamond. Each is given a name, either 'up', 'down', 'right' or 'left', as shown. One player stands in the middle and another is 'spare'.

Up

Play this game quickly and rest after five minutes.

Left

Right

Down

Spare player

The spare player shouts out the names of some of the players. The middle player touches the opposite players – if the spare player shouts 'right, up', the middle player touches 'left, down'. If the middle player gets the instructions right, she changes with the last player touched. If not, she stays in the middle.

QUICK RESPONSE RUNNING

This exercise improves your response times. The faster you can react, the more likely you are to win a race to the ball in a game.

Stand by a row of markers with some teammates, facing a second set of markers 15m (49ft) away. Another player, or your coach, stands nearby and gives instructions.

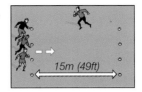

15m (49ft)

Stand in a straight line with your teammates.

1. When your coach shouts 'Now!', start jogging toward the far markers.

As you set off, don't jog too quickly.

2. When your coach shouts 'Down!', sit down as quickly as you can.

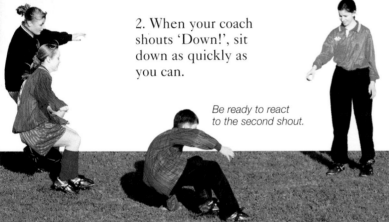

Be ready to react to the second shout.

Try to anticipate the final shout, so that you can get slightly ahead of your teammates.

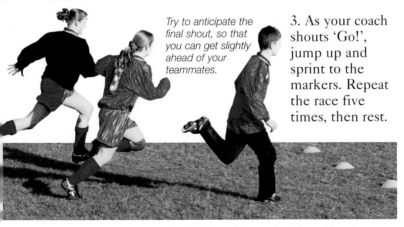

3. As your coach shouts 'Go!', jump up and sprint to the markers. Repeat the race five times, then rest.

REACTION TIPS

★ In the hour or so before you play, try to keep your mind focused on the game ahead.

★ Keep an eye on what is going on around you. Staying alert will help you anticipate play.

This quick-thinking player has intercepted a pass.

★ Once you are focused, you should try to concentrate for the whole game. A brief lapse in concentration can cost your team a goal or the game.

STAR REACTIONS

Here, Italian defender Paulo Maldini is very alert and is quick to challenge an opponent.

GOALKEEPER TRAINING

If you are a goalkeeper, you have a special job to do and a lot of your training needs to be centered around improving your handling, flexibility and strength. Goalies should also have a good level of fitness and need to do running work with their teammates.

ARM AND SHOULDER WORK

This exercise is good for stretching and strengthening your arm and shoulder muscles. If you have strong upper body muscles, it helps improve your catching and punching.

Put one leg slightly in front of you for balance.

A friend stands opposite you about 1m (3ft) away. Lean forward and hold each other's forearms firmly. To loosen and stretch your muscles, both of you rotate your arms, as shown above, slowly building up speed. To strengthen your muscles, take turns pushing against the movement of the other's arms. This makes rotating your arms around much harder to do.

LEG BUILDER

Powerful leg muscles are vital for a goalie, as you often have to jump for crosses and make acrobatic dives. You have to move fast to do this exercise, but it is very effective at building up your leg muscles. You can do this on your own with a ball.

Keep your eyes on the ball all the time.

Stand with your legs 60cm (2ft) apart. Hold a ball in front of you at knee level.

Throw the ball as high as possible into the air and then quickly sit down.

Stand up again before you catch the ball. Do this ten times and then rest.

QUICK PASS GAME

This game works on your basic handling skills and sharpens your reflexes. Holding a ball, stand between two friends who are about 4m (13ft) apart. One of these friends should also have a ball.

Play with other goalies if you can.

Change over after one minute in the middle.

Throw your ball high up into the air, then turn to the friend with a ball.

Catch a throw from this player and quickly turn to your other friend.

Throw the ball to him, and then get ready to catch your own ball again.

MOVE AND DIVE

This game should improve your movement around the goal area and works on your reflexes and flexibility. Mark out a 6m (20ft) wide circle and put six balls an equal distance apart around it. Number them one to six. Stand in the middle of

the circle and ask a friend or another goalie to stand nearby and shout out a number. When your friend shouts, run and dive at this ball. Get up quickly and run back to the center while your friend shouts another number for you to run to.

6m (20ft)

As this game involves a lot of impact with the ground, play on a soft surface. Change over after six saves.

Move around quickly, keeping on your toes.

ON GAME DAYS

On the day of a game, you need a routine for before and after you play. Warm up properly and make sure you keep your muscles warm throughout the game. This helps to prevent injury and stiffness.

A BASIC WARM-UP ROUTINE

A warm-up routine should last ten or fifteen minutes. Start with loosening and stretching exercises. Then do some ball work to give you a feel for the ball and to get you moving around. If you are an attacker, spend some time warming up your goalie by practicing your shooting.

You could use this warm-up routine with a teammate. Put two markers 8m (26ft) apart and stand between them. Each of you has a ball. Both start dribbling toward different markers. Continue around your markers and pass each other in a figure eight movement.

Three minutes of this exercise is enough to warm you up. If you have time, practice passing the ball to each other, too.

Do this routine at a steady pace, with the ball under close control.

RUNNING ROUTINES

The final part of the warm-up should be the most intensive. Spend about five minutes going through a variety of running routines.

Both these routines are used by top players in their pre-game warm-ups.

Start off with some light jogging, before moving on to the techniques shown here. Once you are feeling warm and your muscles are loose, end your warm-up with a couple of fast sprints to get your heart pumping and deepen your breathing.

To work your calf and hamstring muscles, run with your hands held out in front of you. Bring your knees up high so that they touch your hands.

This exercise works your thighs. Run with your hands facing outward behind your back. Bring your heels up high and try to touch your hands.

WHAT TO DO AT HALF TIME

At half time, go into the changing room to rest and keep warm. Have a drink to replace lost fluids and keep doing gentle loosening exercises so you don't get stiff. If you have to spend half time on the field, try to keep moving around and stretching.

This team is spending half time on the field. Each player is doing regular muscle stretches.

SUBSTITUTES

If you are one of your team's substitutes, warm up before a game with your teammates in case you need to replace another player soon after the start. During the game, warm up every ten minutes so that your muscles don't get cold and stiff.

These substitutes are doing a warm-up routine at the edge of the field, in case they are called on to play.

WARMING DOWN AFTER THE GAME

After the game, you should spend a few minutes doing an easy and relaxing warming down session. If you stop exercising suddenly, lactic acid (see page 14) can get trapped in your muscles and can make them feel tired and sore the next day.

Gentle jogging and stretching cools your muscles down slowly and helps to get rid of any lactic acid that has built up.

These players have put on warm clothing and are going through a light warming down session.

PRE- AND POST-GAME TIPS

★ Arrive at a game early so that you have plenty of time to get physically and mentally prepared.

★ Do your warm-up twenty minutes before the start of a game. If you do it too early, your muscles will get cold again and you will have wasted valuable energy.

★ Always build up the intensity of your warm-up gradually. Remember that cold muscles are easily injured, so avoid sudden, explosive movements early on.

★ After a game, have a warm shower. This is good for relaxing your muscles, as well as giving you the chance to get clean.

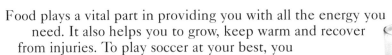

FOOD AND DRINK

Food plays a vital part in providing you with all the energy you need. It also helps you to grow, keep warm and recover from injuries. To play soccer at your best, you need a healthy diet which contains plenty of energy-giving foods.

DIFFERENT KINDS OF FOODS

All food contains some 'nutrients'. Each nutrient helps the body to develop and function in a different way. Carbohydrates, fats, proteins, vitamins and minerals are all nutrients. These are found in different foods in varying amounts.

Most of your energy comes from carbohydrates. Bread, pasta, potatoes, rice and cereals are good carbohydrate sources. Carbohydrates are stored in your liver and muscles as glycogen, or in your blood as glucose.

All these foods are good sources of protein.

Carbohydrate is the main nutrient in these foods.

Sweets also provide you with carbohydrates in the form of sugar (but see opposite page).

Many fruits and vegetables contain vitamins and minerals.

Your body needs vitamins and minerals in small amounts. Many foods contain them. Vitamin C, for instance, which repairs damaged cells and keeps your skin healthy, is found in citrus fruits and green vegetables.

Protein is used to build and repair your body and can also give you energy. Many foods contain some protein but meat, fish, milk, nuts and beans are particularly good sources of it.

Foods containing fat provide energy but you need to do a lot of exercise before you make use of it. Fried foods contain a lot of fat. Meat and dairy products can also contain a high amount of fat.

Butter is almost pure fat. Cakes tend to contain a lot of fat, and red meat can be fatty, too.

WATCHING WHAT YOU EAT

If you eat a balanced diet containing plenty of fresh foods, you should obtain the necessary amounts of protein, vitamins and minerals your body needs each day. Some foods, though, can be bad for you if you eat a lot of them.

Sugar is often added to packaged and canned foods.

Try not to eat too much fatty food as this can lead to heart disease later in life and can make you put on a lot of weight.

Although sugar can give you energy, it contains no other nutrients. A lot of sugar can rot your teeth and may cause pimples.

Packaged snacks and fast foods contain a lot of salt. Too much can cause high blood pressure and blood circulation problems.

WHAT TO DRINK

In a game, sweating makes you lose a lot of fluid. Make sure you replace this fluid quickly or you may become dehydrated. This can lead to cramps (see page 28) and fatigue. Try to drink at regular intervals during play, and also at half time.

You can buy isotonic sports drinks if you don't want to make your own.

Drinks such as tea and coffee are good for making you feel awake and alert but can also dehydrate you. It's best not to drink them just before or after a game.

Water is a good basic drink to have before, during and after a game to keep your fluid levels up. Avoid carbonated water as the gas may make you feel bloated.

As you sweat, you lose salt as well as water. 'Isotonic' drinks give you energy and help your body to replace salt. Water mixed with fruit juice is a good isotonic drink.

EATING TIPS

★ In the two or three days before a game, try to eat more carbohydrate-based food. This helps store up glycogen and glucose and so provides you with more energy when you play.

★ Make sure you have a carbohydrate-based pre-game meal about three or four hours before the game. You need to allow enough time for the food to be digested, or you may feel sick and uncomfortable.

★ Eat another carbohydrate-based meal within a few hours of finishing a game. You will have used up a lot of energy, and you need to replace it as soon as possible. Isotonic drinks will help too.

★ Try to eat a balanced diet all the time to improve and maintain your general health. To get the maximum benefit from your training, it's important that you don't eat too much junk food.

DEALING WITH INJURIES

All soccer players get injured sometimes, whether in a game or as a result of doing a lot of training. Most injuries are not very serious and only take a short time to heal, but you need to know how to treat them, otherwise a small problem can become a big one.

TREATING YOUR OWN INJURIES

Common minor injuries include bruises, cuts or grazes, slight muscle strains and 'sprains' of joints or ligaments (flexible cords that support your joints). If you are not bleeding too much and can still walk, you can treat these yourself. After the game, use an ice pack on bruises, sprains and strains to lessen swelling and pain. Support the injury with a bandage and raise it up on a cushion to keep reducing the swelling.

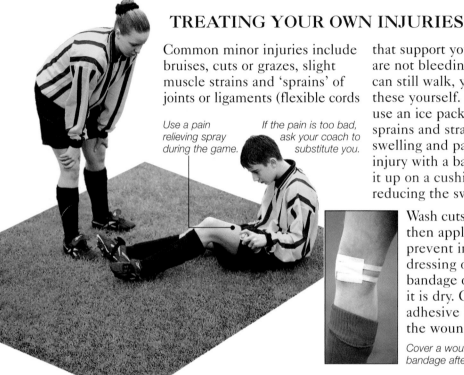

Use a pain relieving spray during the game.

If the pain is too bad, ask your coach to substitute you.

Wash cuts and grazes and then apply antiseptic to prevent infection. Put a dressing or adhesive bandage on the cut once it is dry. Cushioned adhesive bandages give the wound protection.

Cover a wound with an adhesive bandage after cleaning it.

DEALING WITH CRAMPS

Cramps are a very common soccer injury. A cramp involves the painful contraction of a group of muscles. It may be caused by lactic acid in your muscles (see page 14) or by dehydration, so try to drink plenty of fluids during the game.

For cramps in your calf muscle, ask a teammate to straighten your knee and then to gently push your foot up toward your shin.

For cramps in your foot, a teammate gently pushes your toes back. It also helps to stand on the front part, or 'ball', of your foot.

For cramps in your thigh, lie down. Ask someone to straighten your knee and pull your leg up, then push your knee down.

PREVENTING INJURIES

Although there is no guaranteed way of avoiding injury, there are some simple precautions you can take to reduce the chances of it happening. It is important that you look after your body before, during and after a game (see pages 24-25).

You must wear shin pads during a game to protect the lower part of your legs from injury.

Warming up before a game will greatly reduce the risk of pulling a muscle in the first few minutes.

Too much kicking and jumping can damage your knees, so try not to overdo your soccer playing.

SERIOUS INJURIES

When a serious injury occurs, stay calm and get help at once from adults. If a player is in a lot of pain he may have badly pulled or torn a muscle or sprained a joint. Don't try to move him in case he has actually fractured or dislocated a bone or joint. Keep him relaxed, and cover him with a blanket or coat to help him to stay warm.

When a bad injury occurs, stop the game and inform the referee.

The referee should call for medical help.

MAKING A FIRST AID KIT

It is essential for your team to have a bag at every game containing medical products to treat any injuries that occur. Include painkillers to relieve the pain of minor injuries.

Some important things to keep in your bag are a pair of scissors, some adhesive bandages and dressings, antiseptic cream or wipes and pain relieving spray. Try to replace anything you use before the next game.

STAYING FIT AND HEALTHY

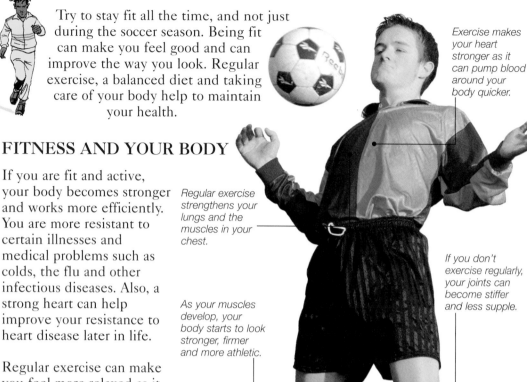

Try to stay fit all the time, and not just during the soccer season. Being fit can make you feel good and can improve the way you look. Regular exercise, a balanced diet and taking care of your body help to maintain your health.

Exercise makes your heart stronger as it can pump blood around your body quicker.

FITNESS AND YOUR BODY

If you are fit and active, your body becomes stronger and works more efficiently. You are more resistant to certain illnesses and medical problems such as colds, the flu and other infectious diseases. Also, a strong heart can help improve your resistance to heart disease later in life.

Regular exercise can make you feel more relaxed as it is an effective way of relieving stress and tension.

Regular exercise strengthens your lungs and the muscles in your chest.

As your muscles develop, your body starts to look stronger, firmer and more athletic.

If you don't exercise regularly, your joints can become stiffer and less supple.

FEELING CONFIDENT

Getting fit can really improve your self confidence. Every time you play a game, you will know that you are as fit, if not fitter, than your opponents. You will be more prepared to attempt difficult challenges and make attacking runs.

Even if you haven't been selected for a team, keep working at your fitness and stay confident. You have a much better chance of being included if you are one of the fittest players in the squad.

This player has the confidence to make an attack on the opposing team's defense.

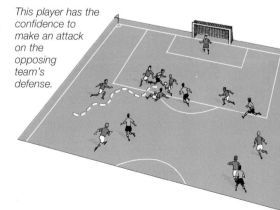

LOOKING AFTER YOURSELF

Although regular exercise is very good for improving your fitness and health, you also need to get plenty of rest. If you make your body do too much work, you may get injured or ill.

If you get a serious injury, you must follow medical advice and take time off to recover. You need to be patient and resume your training schedule slowly. If you do hard physical exercise when you are still injured, you may make the injury even worse.

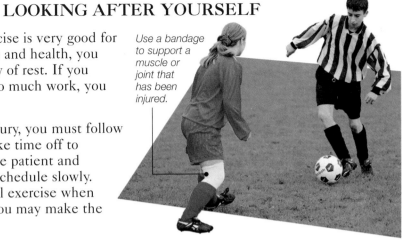

Use a bandage to support a muscle or joint that has been injured.

PRE-SEASON TRAINING

When the soccer season ends, do some form of exercise to maintain your level of fitness. There are many activities to pick from and playing other sports can be fun. You could work out a training schedule including several different sports.

Cycling builds up your leg muscles as well as your stamina. Cycling up hills is particularly hard work.

Tennis is a fun and competitive game. It includes short sprints and works your upper body.

Swimming exercises all your muscles and is excellent for your stamina, strength and suppleness.

STAR PLAYER

Brazilian star Ronaldo is the complete soccer player. He has superb ability and also a high level of fitness.

HEALTH TIPS

★ Keep to a balanced diet, eating plenty of fresh food and fiber and avoiding too much fatty food and sugar.

★ Try to get a good night's sleep every night. Sleep helps your body grow, repair and refresh itself. You need to spend time relaxing your mind and muscles.

★ Avoid addictive substances such as alcohol and cigarettes. These can have a bad effect on your health and can cause serious problems later in life.

★ Once the soccer season is over, try to do a good exercise session about three times a week.

INDEX

Library photographs: Empics
With thanks to Reebok UK

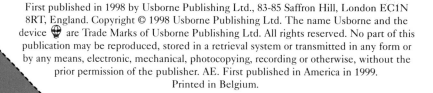